D1525678

SIZZLING Celebrities

Emma!

AMAZING ACTRESS EMMA STONE

BY MICHAEL A. SCHUMAN

Enslow Publishers, Inc.
40 Industrial Road
Box 398
Berkeley Heights, NJ 07922
USA
http://www.enslow.com

Copyright © 2014 by Enslow Publishers, Inc.

Library of Congress Cataloging-in-Publication Data

Schuman, Michael.

    Emma! : amazing actress Emma Stone / Michael A. Schuman.
      pages cm. — (Sizzling celebrities)
    ISBN 978-0-7660-4113-4
    1. Stone, Emma, 1988—Juvenile literature. 2. Actors—United States—Biography—Juvenile literature. 3. Singers—United States—Biography—Juvenile literature. I. Title.
    PN2287.S73S38 2013
    791.4302'8092—dc23
    [B]   2012040314

Future editions:
Paperback ISBN: 978-1-4644-0175-6
EPUB ISBN: 978-1-4645-1088-5
Single-User PDF ISBN: 978-1-4646-1088-2
Multi-User PDF ISBN: 978-0-7660-5716-6

Printed in the United States of America

052013 Lake Book Manufacturing, Inc., Melrose Park, IL

10 9 8 7 6 5 4 3 2 1

To Our Readers: We have done our best to make sure all Internet addresses in this book were active and appropriate when we went to press. However, the author and the publisher have no control over and assume no liability for the material available on those Internet sites or on other Web sites they may link to. Any comments or suggestions can be sent by e-mail to comments@enslow.com or to the address on the back cover.

♻ Enslow Publishers, Inc., is committed to printing our books on recycled paper. The paper in every book contains 10% to 30% post-consumer waste (PCW). The cover board on the outside of each book contains 100% PCW. Our goal is to do our part to help young people and the environment too!

Photo Credits: AP Photo, p. 8; AP Photo/Brad Barket, p. 43; AP Photo/Chris Pizzello, pp. 22, 32, 34, 41; AP Photo/Domenico Stinellis, p. 44; AP Photo/Eric Jamison, p. 38; AP Photo/Jennifer Graylock, pp. 6, 7, 25; AP Photo/Laura Rauch, p. 28; AP Photo/Luis Martinez, p. 19; AP Photo/Matt Sayles pp. 27, 35, 37; AP Photo/Marty Lederhandler, p. 11; AP Photo/Peter Kramer, p. 21; AP Photo/Sony Pictures/Jack Plunkett, p. 31; AP Photo/Vince Bucci, p. 16; Library of Congress, p. 40; Matt Sayles/Invision/AP, pp. 4, 46; Rex Features via AP Images, p. 1.

Cover Photo: Rex Features via AP Images (Emma Stone at *The Croods* film photo shoot at the Berlinale International Film Festival in Germany.)

Contents

CHAPTER 1
The Trailblazer, 5

CHAPTER 2
"She Lived for Performing," 9

CHAPTER 3
Cookies for Dogs, 18

CHAPTER 4
Supergood!, 24

CHAPTER 5
"The Most Unbelievable Thing," 33

Further Info, 47
Index, 48

7

The Trailblazer

On June 3, 2012, actress Emma Stone attended the MTV Movie Awards. She was nominated in two categories for her role in a romantic comedy titled *Crazy, Stupid, Love.* While she won no awards for the movie, she did win a special honor.

The category was a new one: the MTV Trailblazer Award. Older similar shows, such as the Academy Awards, give out lifetime achievement awards for actors who have earned respect for starring in dozens of movies in their long lives. But the Academy Awards date to the 1920s when the movie industry was young.

The first MTV Movie Awards presentation was in 1992. The MTV Movie Awards also tend to get a much younger audience than the Academy Awards. So it makes sense that their award categories are of more interest to younger people.

Instead of a lifetime achievement award, MTV decided to give a special award to a young actor. According to MTV, the purpose of the MTV Trailblazer Award is to honor an actor who does a wide variety of movies and cannot be typecast, or

◄ *Emma Stone accepts the Trailblazer Award at the MTV Movie Awards on Sunday, June 3, 2012, in Los Angeles.*

expected to play the same type of role in every movie. For example, Adam Sandler has been very successful making funny movies. He has made a few serious movies, but he is best known for his silly ones.

Emma Stone started out making comedies, but then she starred in a smash movie about the civil rights era titled *The Help*. It drew a large number of moviegoers and most critics loved it. It offered proof that Stone could not be typecast. The fact that this was MTV's first Trailblazer Award meant something special.

As she stood in front of an audience of actors and other important movie industry people, Stone got teary eyed. She said, "Thank you, I'm a crier."

She then went on to say, "So, I looked up the actual definition of 'trailblazer,' and it means someone who blazes a trail to be followed by others. And that's an honor to hear you're being associated with a concept like that. But the only thing I can hope that an award inspires is originality."

The cast of The Help at the 18th Annual Screen Actors Guild Awards. From left to right: Sissy Spacek, Mary Steenburgen, Ahna O'Reilly, Mike Vogel, Cicely Tyson, Jessica Chastain, Chris Lowell, Emma Stone, Octavia Spencer, Allison Janney, Viola Davis.

She then went on to list actors, an author (J. D. Salinger), and musicians (the Beatles) who inspired her. Stone said, "Those people are my creative trailblazers, but I'm not following any of their paths, and what's incredible about them is they help make me want to be more myself because they're all originals."

Stone concluded, "But that you'll continue to harness your own originality and what makes you unique 'cause I know that when you're a teenager—and sometimes when you're an adult—what sets you apart can sometimes feel like a burden and it's not. And a lot of the time, it's what makes you great." She then took her seat to a loud round of applause.

Steve Martin (right), John Candy (left), and director John Hughes during a press conference for Planes, Trains and Automobiles *in 1987.*

"She Lived for Performing"

Emily Jean Stone was born in the desert city of Scottsdale, Arizona, on November 6, 1988. She was a blonde-haired baby who whined and cried a lot. Part of the reason for her crankiness is that she suffered from severe colic. Colic is a condition that affects the digestive system. It is especially hard on infants. Stone said, "My mom dealt with a screaming baby 24 hours a day for first six months of my life. I screamed myself hoarse every day and developed nodules [masses of tissue in the body] as an infant. So I have calluses on my vocal cords [to this day]."

Her father was a builder while her mother stayed home and raised the family. Emma has a younger brother named Spencer. It was her father who turned her on to movies. He loved silly comedies, such as Steve Martin's *The Jerk*. It was the first movie she ever saw. She and her father also loved another comedy, *Planes, Trains and Automobiles*, which starred John Candy and Steve Martin.

She said that because her father watched the movies over and over, she watched them many times, too. There is a scene in *Planes, Trains and Automobiles* in which Steve Martin's character loses his temper in an airport and swears repeatedly. Stone admitted she had that dialogue memorized as a child. Her mother was disgusted to hear her use that language but her father thought it was a big joke. She said of those classic comedies, "I loved them and my dad loved them, and we would laugh together, and I would think, 'This is love. I just wanted to make people feel like that.'"

Her father also introduced her to the television comedy show *Saturday Night Live.* Her favorite regular actor on *Saturday Night Live* was Gilda Radner. Because Radner left the show before Emily was born, Stone must have seen her in reruns. Classic episodes of *Saturday Night Live* are shown on cable television channels. Her favorite Radner character was a teenage girl who acted out short plays in her bedroom. Stone used to do the same thing. She dreamed of some day being a guest host on *Saturday Night Live.*

When she was seven, Emily took gymnastic lessons. One day she was standing on the parallel bars and the woman supporting her let go of her ankles. Emily fell forward and broke both her arms on the mat. As a result, for the next two years Emily suffered from panic attacks. She was anxious and nervous much of the time. Stone recalled, "I had massive anxiety as a child. I was in therapy. From 8 to 10, I was borderline agoraphobic. [Agoraphobia is a condition in which a person is afraid to be in public places.] I could not leave my mom's side."

She said that acting helped her overcome her fears. In her childhood days, she attended Sequoya Elementary School. Then for one year—sixth grade—she attended another public

Part of the cast of Saturday Night Live *in 1978. From left: cast member Jane Curtin, guest host Chevy Chase, and cast members Bill Murray, Gilda Radner, and Laraine Newman.*

school, Cocopah Middle School. Stone remembered, "I made sure I got all A's. It was weird. I didn't like school at all, but I could not get a B. ... Whatever I could control at that time, I felt like I needed to control, which I don't feel like so much anymore."

One day her mother drove Emily into Arizona's busy capital city, Phoenix. There, Emily hoped to try out for a children's theater troupe called Valley Youth Theatre. At age eleven, she showed up with a photo of herself and a small resume, or a list of her talents. Valley Youth Theatre accepted her.

Soon she was a regular. In addition to performing plays, Valley Youth Theatre has an improvisational comedy group. Improvisation, or improv, is a form of comedy acting in which the actors don't have set lines memorized. Instead they make up funny lines on the spot.

She said that acting "made me feel great. I started doing improv the year after my tough two years [in which she suffered from agoraphobia]. It helped."

By then Stone knew all she wanted to do was act. The first play she auditioned, or tried out, for was *The Wind in the Willows* at age eleven. The play was based on a classic children's book written by Kenneth Grahame in 1908. The main characters are forest animals who take on humanlike qualities. Emily played the role of Otter. As part of her costume she wore a fake hairy chest, which was one of the most memorable moments of the play for the audience, the cast, and the staff.

Her acting teacher, Bobb Cooper, remembered how she spoke in a deep, raspy voice. It was deep because of the nodules she developed in her throat when she was a baby. Cooper also remembered, "She really knew how to project. She was very loud."

Over the next few years, she acted in improv and fifteen more children's plays, such as *The Princess and the Pea*, *Cinderella*, and *Alice in Wonderland*.

Cooper remembered that Emily stood out among the other actors. He said, "She was a cut-up, she liked to talk and crack jokes, and be funny. The more she was here the more comfortable she became and the more vocal. There were no boyfriends that I remember but she had a lot of very close friends. She wasn't a girly girl." She did not like to wear dresses. Most of the time, she showed up to her classes in jeans.

Stone auditioned for every play Valley Youth Theatre produced. Cooper recalled, "She talked a lot about wanting to be a star, she was always so driven and she lived for performing. She was very talented, she was doing show after show, after show. She was so good it was hard not to cast her and the great thing about Emma was she was willing to play anything."

Cooper also noted, "Of course, anyone can dream, but not anyone can be a star. We help them [the student actors] understand that it takes dedication, teamwork, and hard work. You have to stay focused on your goal."

She was so driven by the acting bug that she asked her parents for a very special favor. After she completed sixth grade, she asked to be homeschooled. That means her parents would teach her at home. She could then have a flexible schedule, which would give her ample time to go to auditions. Her parents agreed. It seemed she spent most of her waking hours over the next two years at Valley Youth Theatre. Then she spent her freshman year in high school at all-female Catholic high school called Xavier College Preparatory.

But traditional school was not for her. By that time she had her eyes set on a huge goal. It would take a lot of courage and a lot of convincing of her parents.

One evening when she was fifteen, Emily made a batch of popcorn and asked her parents to watch a PowerPoint presentation she created. She called it "Project Hollywood 2004" and set it to a Madonna song titled "Hollywood." In a nutshell, the song is about people moving to Los Angeles to try to be successful in the movie industry. The song is also about how people think life in Hollywood is glamorous—even though in real life it is not often that way.

Using the PowerPoint presentation, Emily wanted to convince them to let her drop out of Xavier College Preparatory School and try to make a career in the movie industry. Her PowerPoint presentation featured photographs of performers who started acting when they were young and became successful. Her point was that it would be better for her to try now rather than wait until she graduated from high school.

It was certainly a bold move. Every month thousands of would-be actors move to Los Angeles and New York City to try to break into show business. Most of them have to take jobs as food servers, delivery people, or car parking attendants to earn money while they audition for roles. There are many more people looking for work as actors than there are acting jobs. Some eke out a living acting in minor roles in movies, television commercials, or in small parts on live stage. Others never get jobs as actors and spend their lives doing odd jobs. Very few become mega-stars.

In a way, Emily had it a bit easier than adults trying to break into acting. Her parents agreed to let her give it a shot, but only if her mother would live with her in California. Her parents would take care of her expenses so she would not have to worry about getting a job. In fact, she was so young she would have to finish school. She planned to have her mother homeschool her again. She also took online courses.

Emily's mother knew how much this meant to her. But she wanted to make sure Emily was not entering this adventure blindly. They would not let Emily make her move without knowing more about the ins and outs of the acting profession.

EMMA!

Emma's parents would not let her go to Hollywood without an agent. Here, Emma and her mother, Krista, arrive at the 18th Annual Screen Actors Guild Awards in 2012. ▶

First of all, they would not let her go to Los Angeles until she had an agent. It is very unusual for an actor to get a professional job without an agent. The agent's job is to represent the actor. In other words, if a movie is going to be made and Justin Timberlake's agent thinks he would be perfect for a part, he would call Timberlake and tell him about it. Timberlake would say whether he wanted or did not want to try out for the part. If Timberlake wanted to, then his agent would arrange for Timberlake to audition for the role. Of course, he would be competing against other actors.

16

Emily's mother found an acting coach who had once worked for the William Morris Agency. The William Morris Agency is one of the most famous acting agencies. This acting coach knew people in the movie industry. At first, the coach thought Emily overacted, or tried too hard to get herself into a role. She told Emily to tone her acting down a little. She gave Emily lessons. Once the coach felt Emily had improved enough to work as a professional, she called some agents she knew in Los Angeles.

Emily and her mother flew to Los Angeles a few times for auditions. In her earliest auditions, Emily acted the same two roles. One was a monologue from the hit teen comedy movie *Clueless*. It had come out in 1995. Another part of her audition was a part from a dramatic movie. But by 2011 she had forgotten what it was.

Cookies for Dogs

After trying out for different agencies, Emily was finally hired by one named the Savage Agency. It is owned by a woman named Judy Savage, whose specialty is teen actors. Some of the young actors Savage has worked with include Academy Award winner Hilary Swank, Danica McKellar from the 1980s hit television program *The Wonder Years*, and Alyson Michalka, who acted in the Disney Channel television series *Phil of the Future*.

Emily and her mother permanently moved to Los Angeles, and the Savage Agency sent Emily out on constant auditions. She tried out repeatedly for eight months for roles in programs like those on the Disney Channel. Yet she had nothing to show for all her efforts. Stone remembered, "I went up for every single show on the Disney Channel and auditioned to play the daughter on every single sitcom." "Sitcom" is short for "situation comedy" or a comedy television program that features the same actors in the same roles every week.

The agency lost interest in her and stopped sending Emily to auditions. To fill her time she took a job at a bakery that made cookies for dogs. It looked like Emily might be one of those would-be actors who had to work odd jobs. She admitted she was horrible as a cookie maker. Three customers even said their dogs would not eat the cookies she had made.

But Emily refused to quit. At one point it seemed like she was going to get a break and be on a television series. It all started when her mother saw a commercial on the VH1 television network for actors for a new teen-centered reality show.

In 1970, a television sitcom about a family pop music group called *The Partridge Family* premiered. The members of the Partridge family were mainly unrelated actors playing a family. However, two actors were partially related. The mother was played by Shirley Jones and her son was played by her real-life stepson

Emma Stone arrives at the Brandon Davis Jean by Replay launch party on April 24, 2006, in Hollywood. ▶

David Cassidy. The fictional family consisted of the mother, three sons, and two daughters. One daughter, the teenage Laurie Partridge, was played by actor Susan Dey. She played keyboards in the fictional group.

When Emily's mother saw the commercial for a reality contest for *The New Partridge Family*, she told her daughter that she looked like Susan Dey. Maybe, she thought, Emily could try out for Laurie, the part that Dey played on the original *The Partridge Family*.

The New Partridge Family was planned to begin as a contest reality show. Actors would audition for the roles, and winners would be chosen. Then the producers would videotape a pilot episode, or test episode, for the new series. *The New Partridge Family* auditions were arranged as part of an open call. That means actors did not have to have agents to try out for roles.

Emily was not excited about playing a fake musician on *The New Partridge Family*. Yet she tried out at her mother's urging. After several weeks, she won the role of Laurie. Even though she was not thrilled about her first part, this proved to her parents that her gamble of trying to become an actor was starting to pay off.

The pilot episode was videotaped. For some reason, people did not take to it. The television executives did not pick it up to be a regular series. Emily was once more without an acting job.

Emma would eventually star in movies with Anna Faris and Penn Badgley. Here, Emma and Anna promote The House Bunny.

The New Partridge Family adventure was not a total loss. She got to meet and know producer and manager Doug Wald. While an agent's main job is to try to get roles for an actor, a manager takes care of the actor's business matters. Sometimes the agent's and manager's jobs overlap. Wald already was the manager for well-known actor Anna Faris, as well as Penn Badgley of the television series *Gossip Girl*.

Wald got Emily guest-starring roles on already existing sitcoms. In a guest role, Emily would not appear weekly in a regular part. Instead she appeared in just one episode. Some programs she appeared on included *Malcolm in the Middle*, *Medium*, and *The Suite Life of Zack and Cody*.

Now that she was getting professional jobs, Emily had to join the Screen Actors Guild (SAG). SAG is a union, or a group of workers in a profession. There are unions for workers in all kinds of jobs, including teachers, carmakers, and electricians.

Emma was disappointed when she was not cast in Heroes. *Hayden Panettiere poses with her fellow* Heroes *castmates, Greg Grunberg, Jack Coleman, and Santiago Cabrera at the 64th Annual Golden Globe Awards.*

The purpose of the union is to make sure that workers are treated fairly by their bosses.

When Emily applied for SAG membership, she learned that there was already an actor—though not a famous one—named Emily Stone. So Emily simply changed her stage name to Emma. Her friends and family still call her by her given name, Emily. But to the rest of the world, she would from then on be known as Emma.

Her guest roles led to an audition for a regular series. It was a science-fiction drama called *Heroes*, where ordinary people discover they have super powers. Emma was auditioning for the part of high school cheerleader Claire Bennet. She wanted the role with all her heart. As Stone waited for her chance to audition, she could hear a girl auditioning in a nearby room. She overheard the directors tell the other girl, "You are our pick... On a scale of 1 to 10, you're an 11."

Stone saw the other girl walk out of the audition room. It was Hayden Panettiere. Panettiere was already well known. She had started as a child actor in afternoon soap operas. She then had a recurring role in *Malcolm in the Middle*. She had also appeared in the movies *Remember the Titans*, *Raising Helen*, *Ice Princess*, and *Racing Stripes*.

Stone remembered she did not take the rejection well. "I went home and just had this meltdown." She said she felt it was the "rock bottom" moment of her life.

Yet auditions continued. Shortly after losing the part in *Heroes*, Emma got what she wanted: a job on a regular weekly show. It was an adventure drama called *Drive*, broadcast on the Fox television network. *Drive* first aired in April 2007. The running plot was about an illegal crosscountry road race. A total of six episodes were made but only four were shown before *Drive* was canceled. That meant *Drive* would not be aired on television anymore. *Drive* did not get the ratings, or numbers of viewers, that Fox network executives has hoped for.

Another important person Emma met through her activity in the entertainment industry was Allison Jones. Jones is a casting director. While an agent works for an actor, a casting director works for people making a movie or a play. The casting director looks for the best actors to play certain parts.

Shortly after *Drive* was canceled, Jones thought Stone would be a good fit for a role in a raunchy teenage comedy called *Superbad*. It was not yet definite that *Superbad* would even be made. Yet producer Judd Apatow wanted to go ahead and cast actors for it. Jones thought Stone should try out for the part

Emma Stone attends the ▶ *world premiere of* I Now Pronounce You Chuck & Larry *in 2007.*

of Jules, an attractive girl whom a geeky, chubby boy, played by Jonah Hill, has a crush on.

Stone read the script and liked it right away. She said, "The script was so hysterical to me so I was just excited to be a part of something that was funny and in line with my humor because that's so rare." She also got the chance to do some improv with Hill during the audition. That is unusual, but Stone was excited about the opportunity.

When the audition was over, Stone said she felt she was "terrible." But she was about the only person who felt so. She got the role. However, producer Apatow wanted Stone to make one change. He thought that with her blonde hair Stone looked too much like a typical cheerleader in teen movies. He felt she would be more appealing as a redhead. So Stone dyed her hair red.

An even bigger surprise was the audiences' and critics' reactions to *Superbad*. Raunchy teenage movies are a dime a dozen. They usually are cheap to make and rely heavily on slapstick, gross-out humor, and a lot of swear words. Some critics have said they are so similar that if you have seen one teen movie, you have seen them all.

But *Superbad* was different. Critics and audiences loved it. The movie was released on August 17, 2007. It was an immediate hit. The movie cost $20 million to make. That might sound like a lot of money, but in the world of making movies, it is very little. Word got out that *Superbad* was so entertaining that it made more money in its first weekend in the theaters—over $33 million—than it cost to make.

Superbad went on to earn over $121 million in the United States alone. It also made over $48 million more in foreign countries, for a grand total worldwide of nearly $170 million.

What made *Superbad* so different from other similar teenage comedies? Critics felt the movie may have had its share of dirty jokes and disgusting humor, but it also had heart. It captured the characters' true feelings, and that made it seem very real. Kevin Williamson, the movie critic for the *Toronto (Ontario) Sun*, wrote, "*Superbad* is super-awesome—a miracle of crudeness and charm that counters its coarseness with sincerity" and that the production staff "have made one of the filthiest, sweetest movies in memory."

Emma's first major role was in Superbad. *Here, she arrives at the premiere in 2007.* ▶

Stone got roles in more movies but was always cast as a supporting actor, or someone who plays a background part. Her next movie was *The Rocker*. It starred Rainn Wilson from the television sitcom *The Office*. Wilson plays a washed-up drummer trying to make a comeback in a much younger rock band. Emma is the bass player. Her character, Amanda, is a gloomy girl. Emma had no idea how to play bass before she was hired. She took bass lessons and joked about her newfound talent when the movie had completed filming. Stone said she could play all eight songs from the movie as well as the Beatles' classic song *Day Tripper*.

She added that playing the moody bass player in *The Rocker* was difficult because her real personality is so different. "It's an interesting part to play because in my life, I'm a big laugher and smiler, so it was an interesting challenge, but definitely a cool one." Offscreen, she had a real-life romance with one of the actors. Teddy Geiger, who is just two months older than Stone, played a guitarist. But like the movie, after a while the romance fizzled.

The Rocker had more or less been forgotten after it was released in 2008. Critics' reviews were mixed. The same was

Cast members Jane Lynch, left, Emma Stone, Lonny Ross, Rainn Wilson, and Fred Armisen arrive at the premiere of The Rocker.

true for the moviegoers. Overall, the movie lost money. It cost $15 million to make and earned back less than $9 million worldwide.

Stone's next two movies were similar comedies. One was titled *The House Bunny*, which was released in 2008. The other was *Ghosts of Girlfriends Past*, which came out the next year. The critics and audiences gave them mixed reviews, although *The House Bunny* was the better liked of the two. Even though she was making movies regularly, she admitted that she had another goal in mind—one from her childhood. In 2008 she told *Access Hollywood* magazine, "My dream is to be on *Saturday Night Live*. And that dream has not faded away."

Emma's acting skills continued to impress movie producers. She had two more movies released in 2009. One, *Zombieland*, is a combination horror/comedy. That is an unusual combination, but it worked. The basic plot is about a few humans who try to escape zombies who have taken over Earth. Stone plays a con artist.

Zombieland was not a super hit, but both critics and audiences liked it. Stone's role was new for her. She explained, "It's been really fun and really different to learn to shoot guns and to try and look tough. I've never really played a woman before. I've only really played girls. This [character] is very much a woman. It's interesting. It's really cool. It's been a huge challenge more so than I thought it would be."

Her work on *Zombieland* impressed two well-known and respected actors, Woody Harrelson and Bill Murray. Murray had gotten his big break on Stone's favorite television show, *Saturday Night Live*. That was twelve years before she was born. Harrelson told the *London Independent*, "I remember being with Bill Murray on *Zombieland*. He was like, 'That girl is just gold—everything that comes out of her mouth. An incredible improviser.' It's really rare that you see a really funny beautiful woman, who really just has the total package."

Her next movie was produced in 2009 but came out in 2010. The title was *Paper Man*. It was a complete turnaround from *Zombieland*. *Paper Man* is an offbeat comedy/drama—more drama than comedy—in which Stone had her biggest role so far. She plays a teenage girl who helps a middle-aged writer find purpose in his life. Yet there is no romance between the two. They are just friends. The friendship works because he is immature for his age and she is mature for her age.

Paper Man was made on a small budget and made very little money. It played mainly in independent theaters. Independent theaters often show movies that are inexpensive to make. Multiplex theaters mostly show big blockbusters that cost hundreds of millions of dollars to make. Many critics felt *Paper Man* was confusing, and most did not like it.

But there was one scene in which Stone stood out. Her character is supposed to run into the Atlantic Ocean in the middle of winter. It was actually the middle of November when

Actors Woody Harrelson (right), Emma Stone, and Jesse Eisenberg attend an advance screening of the film Zombieland at Fantastic Fest in Austin, Texas, in 2009.

the scene was shot. The temperature was in the 30s. Stone recalled, "They actually had a stunt double for me, the same woman who was my stunt double on *Zombieland*, but I ended up doing it myself. It was important for me to feel that cold, because that's what the character was experiencing."

In the fall of 2009, Emma Stone left Los Angeles and moved to New York City. The more famous she became, the more people

◄ *Emma Stone arrives at the MTV Video Music Awards on September 12, 2010, in Los Angeles.*

recognized her. Paparazzi, photographers who take photos of famous people, began to bother her in Los Angeles. She told reporter Alexandra Wolfe, "Once I didn't have to be there anymore I came here." She added, "I actually like L.A. a lot more now that I don't have to live there." Still, she spent a lot of time flying from coast to coast. She still had to go to Los Angeles to shoot films.

Stone did not actually appear in her next movie. She did the voice of a dog named Mazie in the animated/live-action film *Marmaduke*, released in 2010. It is based on the newspaper comic strip about an out-of-control Great Dane. *Marmaduke* entertained families in the summer of 2010 but was then quickly forgotten. But something much bigger was waiting for Stone: her first lead role.

"The Most Unbelievable Thing"

Stone got hold of a script for a movie called *Easy A*. It is about a nice high school girl named Olive Penderghast who gets trapped by a lie that she tells her best friend. Soon, things spiral out of control, her reputation gets damaged, and others at school cause many unforseen complications.

Easy A scriptwriter Bert V. Royal based the story loosely on the Nathaniel Hawthorne classic novel *The Scarlet Letter*. Hawthorne's book is about a woman who commits adultery in colonial America. Royal changed the setting to a high school in 2010 and greatly changed the plot.

Stone liked the story from the first time she read it. She said, "It's so different and unique from anything I'd read before. There are so many messages throughout it, but it is not speaking down to anybody. It's not a message movie. It's funny and sweet."

The man hired to direct the movie was Will Gluck. Stone wasted no time in meeting with Gluck to talk to him about playing the role of Olive. As soon as auditions started, Emma told reporter Sheila Roberts, "I tried to be in there first. I was really crazy about it. And I'm happy that we're sitting here talking about this movie and that I got to be a part of it." Critics and audiences loved *Easy A*.

According to the Web site Rotten Tomatoes, 85 percent of critics liked it. A total of 75 percent of audiences liked it. Several compared it to classic teen movies such as *Mean Girls* and *Heathers*. Many critics credited the movie's success to Stone's acting. Richard Corliss, a movie reviewer for *Time* magazine, wrote, "As for Emma Stone, she didn't have to win me over.

Easy A cast members Patricia Clarkson, Emma Stone, Penn Badgley, Aly Michalka, and Dan Byrd (l-r) pose together at the premiere on September 13, 2010.

Actress Emma Stone arrives at the Golden Globe Awards on January 16, 2011. She was nominated for Best Actress in a Motion Picture Musical or Comedy for Easy A.

She conquered me from the first A." Lisa Kennedy, critic for the *Denver Post*, wrote, "A gem of a turn by Emma Stone as high school student Olive Penderghast makes this tale of a girl, gossip and independence a smart and self-aware hoot in the tradition of the teen flicks of the 1980s."

Stone's acting ability earned her a nomination for the Golden Globe Award for Best Actress in a Motion Picture Musical or Comedy. She did not win the Golden Globe, but she did win an MTV Movie Award for Best Comedic Performance. She also finally achieved her biggest dream. Stone was now a big enough star to be selected as a guest host on *Saturday Night Live.* She told Adam Markovitz of *Entertainment Weekly,* "The number-one highlight of my entire life has been hosting *SNL* [in

October 2010]. That was my ultimate dream. I can't ever top that. I'm just coasting through the rest of my life."

Of course, someone as energetic as Emma Stone could never coast through life. She was getting a reputation as a go-to actor for romantic comedies. In 2011, she costarred in two such films. One was titled *Friends with Benefits*, in which she has a minor role. The other was *Crazy, Stupid, Love*. Both received good reviews and were popular with audiences. Also, both made profits for their studios. *Crazy, Stupid, Love* was the more successful of the two.

In *Crazy, Stupid, Love*, Stone turned a corner in her acting image. She was past the point of mainly playing teenagers. She was twenty-three years old and played the part of an adult—a female lawyer. But while making the movie she had a horrible experience. There is a scene in which her costar Ryan Gosling has to lift Emma over his head while they are dancing. As the scene was being filmed, Stone had a flashback to the time she was dropped at age seven during a gymnastics class. She had a panic attack, feeling as if she might be dropped again. She tried the scene a second time, but with the same result.

Stone told television host Jay Leno, "It just kept happening and I had to go lay down for like an hour" until the panic went away. Leno's audience started laughing because they thought she was exaggerating. Stone responded, "It's not funny. It's very scary." Emma could not finish the scene. A stunt double did it for her.

Emma Stone, with Crazy, Stupid, Love *castmates Steve Carell, left, and Ryan Gosling, presents the award for best villain at the MTV Movie Awards on June 5, 2011.*

Stone was now well known for playing romantic comic roles. That was about to change. She was offered the lead role in a drama set during the civil rights movement era, the early 1960s.

It is called *The Help*, and is adapted from a best-selling 2009 book by Kathryn Stockett. Stockett grew up in Mississippi in the early 1960s. She based the book partly on her own life. Stockett was a young girl in a white family that hired

African-American maids and nannies to clean their house and look after their children.

But the maids were often treated poorly. Some white home owners would not even let the maids use their bathrooms. In Stockett's book, the hero is a girl who just graduated college and works as a journalist. Her name is Eugenia "Skeeter" Phelan. Skeeter decides to write a book on how poorly the maid and nannies are treated.

Mississippi was a segregated state at the time. Laws kept whites and blacks from using the same public drinking fountains, hotels, and bathrooms. As a result of the book, a lot of white people in her

The Help actors, from ▶ left, Viola Davis, Emma Stone, Octavia Spencer, and Bryce Dallas Howard, pose for a portrait backstage at CinemaCon in 2011.

town instantly dislike Skeeter for stirring up trouble between the races.

In 2010, Stone called her mother to tell her she was going to try out for a role from a book called *The Help*. Though Stone had not read *The Help*, her mother had, and she loved it. Her mother was thrilled. Stone recalled, "She screamed in my ear and proceeded to tell me that 'Oh my God, this is the most unbelievable thing that's ever happened to you! Do you realize the weight of this?!'"

Stone then met *The Help* director Tate Taylor. Taylor said he wanted Skeeter to be played by a female actor who reminded him of actor Joan Cusack when she was twenty-two. (Joan Cusack has been acting for decades and was by then nearly fifty.) The character Skeeter is not a beauty like other characters Stone had previously played. She has frizzy hair and is awkward.

As soon as Taylor met Stone, he was overwhelmed. Taylor said, "Emma was completely awkward and dorky, with her raspy voice ... We had a blast and I thought, 'Good God! This is Skeeter.'" The book's author, Kathryn Stockett, next met with Stone and Taylor. Stockett approved Taylor's decision. Stone had to work with a dialect coach to help her develop a Southern accent that sounded real.

Stone knew little about the civil rights movement. She ordered books and DVDs on the subject and studied them. One

Martin Luther King, Jr., was a very important part of the civil rights movement.

documentary was titled *Eyes on the Prize* and it lasts several hours. She wondered why the public schools she attended limited civil rights history to Martin Luther King, Jr., and Rosa Parks, an African-American woman who played a major role in the movement in the 1950s.

Stone remarked, "I don't know how it was so shocking to me to see *Eyes on the Prize*, the documentary series, to see the things that were happening. It was like, how did I not know this?"

To be as realistic as possible, *The Help* was filmed in rural Mississippi. In fact, Stone was in the middle of a Mississippi cotton field when she received a call that she had been hired to play a much sought-after role: Gwen Stacy, in the movie *The Amazing Spider-Man*, which would begin filming soon.

But first, she finished making *The Help*. It opened in movie theaters on August 10, 2011. Being a serious drama with a touch of light comedy, it drew audiences that don't go to teen movies or romantic comedies. Emma Stone became a household name. It also got her a second gig hosting *Saturday Night Live.*

The Help made a ton of money. It cost $25 million to make and earned over $211 million. Most critics raved about it, and it earned an Academy Award nomination for Best Picture of the year. (It did not win, though.)

Critics generally praised Stone's performance. Peter Travers of *Rolling Stone* magazine wrote, "Skeeter is a tricky part ... but Stone, an exceptional talent, is so subtly effective at showing Skeeter's naivete."

Emma Stone accepts ▶ *the award for Favorite Movie Actress for Crazy, Stupid, Love during the People's Choice Awards on January 11, 2012.*

Entertainment Weekly's Owen Gleiberman raved about her: "I've loved Stone as a wide-eyed comic sprite, but here playing a young woman more no-nonsense than anyone around her, she doesn't just sparkle—she holds the movie together." But not all critics praised Stone. Meghan Keane of the *New York Observer* said, "… the raspy voice and adorable delivery that served her well in light teen films like *Easy A* and *Superbad* just aren't enough. She is in far over her head here."

Her fans felt it was an insult that she did not get nominated for an Academy Award for Best Actress. However, she did win two 2012 People's Choice awards—for Favorite Actress and Favorite Comedic Actress. Academy Award winners are selected by people in the movie industry. The winners of the People's Choice awards are selected by fans. Because of that, critics tend not to take them as seriously as the Academy Awards. But her two People's Choice awards proved that she has a huge number of faithful fans.

Despite her busy schedule making one movie after another, Stone has found time to do volunteer work. She is very active in a charity called Stand Up To Cancer. Her mother is a cancer survivor. Stone also appeared in November 2011 at a fund-raising event for a group called Worldwide Orphans Foundation (WWO). The group helps improve the lives of orphaned children around the world.

She also discussed other favorite projects. "I really love a non-profit [charity] called Little Projects. It helps with

Will Arnett, Amy Poehler, and Emma Stone attend the Worldwide Orphans Foundation's Seventh Annual Benefit Gala in New York, on November 14, 2011.

homelessness and getting school supplies to kids who need them. I love Gilda's Club, a charity created in memory of Gilda Radner, a place where people affected by cancer can go for free ... My mom was always a big supporter of volunteer work. My dad has a non-profit called Summit Charity. My parents always felt it was very important, so since I was a kid, it's always been at the forefront of my family's minds."

Actors Andrew Garfield and Emma Stone pose during a photo call for The Amazing Spider-Man *in Rome, on June 22, 2012.*

Her busy schedule has caused her to drop some leisure activities. She stopped using Facebook when she said she "got addicted to Farmville." She exercises by rock climbing but doesn't overdo it. Stone had to do weight training to get ready for her role as Gwen Stacy in *The Amazing Spider-Man*. She found that all it did was get her angry.

While the weight room was not her favorite place to spend time, filming *Spider-Man* was a pleasure, especially because it was filmed in New York City. Stone said, "*Spiderman* [sic] was the first time I've worked in New York since living here. It was the first time I got to stay in my apartment during work, not at a hotel, so that was nice." And she laughed, "And I got to have my New York bagels while working! And my New York cheesecake."

She also had the fun of playing Gwen as a blonde. After appearing with dyed red hair since *Superbad*, audiences believed she was a natural redhead. "My hair is naturally blonde, so it's kind of nice. I look in the mirror and say, 'Oh my God, it's me again, it's been so long.'" She added that she had been a redhead for so long that sometimes she felt as if she were wearing a blonde wig.

Even though Stone does not like to talk about her private life, it soon became known that she and *Spider-Man* costar Andrew Garfield were dating. He called her Em and she called him Garfy. But neither felt their dating life was the public's business. Garfield said, "We don't talk about anything personal. That's just the way it is. Right now, we're just actors."

The Amazing Spider-Man opened on July 3, 2012. It was an expensive movie to make, at $240 million. But within two weeks it more than made that money back. It was enjoyed by critics, too. According to Rotten Tomatoes, seventy-three percent of the critics who reviewed it liked it. Critic Claudia Puig of *USA Today* said one of the reasons the movie is so good is its stars. Puig wrote, "The casting of Garfield as Spidey and Emma Stone as Gwen Stacy is inspired. He's appealingly awkward and boyishly handsome. She's radiant and self-assured."

◄ *Emma Stone attends the LA premiere of* Gangster Squad *at TCL Chinese Theatre.*

Stone has not slowed down. She appeared in two movies in 2013 that were totally opposite from one another. The first was a violent crime drama titled *Gangster Squad*. It was directed by Ruben Fleischer, who directed *Zombieland*. The second was an animated family feature, *The Croods*. As in *Marmaduke*, Stone is heard but not seen. She does the voice of the teenager of a prehistoric family that goes on a risky adventure.

Her movie roles prove one thing—Stone is nothing if not versatile, and will surely be in demand for great roles for years to come.

Further Info

Books

Dabrowski, Kristen. *My First Monologue Book: 100 Monologues for Young Children*: My First Acting Series. Portland, Maine: Smith & Kraus, 2007.

Swenson, Alex. *33 Kids Monologues: Acting School Stop*. Kindle edition, Amazon.com, 2011.

Internet Addresses

Internet Movie Database
<http://www.imdb.com/name/nm1297015/ >

***People* Magazine**
<http://www.people.com/people/emma_stone/0,,,00.html>

Index

A

acting
acting coaches, 17
agents, 16–17, 21
auditions, 12, 13, 17, 18, 20, 23–25
casting directors, 24
drama, 6, 37–42
guest roles, 21–22
Hollywood move, 13–15
improvisation (improv), 12, 13, 25
inspirations, 8–10
managers, 21
romantic comedies, 29, 35–36
sitcoms, 18, 20–22
Valley Youth Theatre, 12–14
The Amazing Spider-Man, 40, 44–45
awards, honors, 5–8, 35, 41, 42

C

charity work, 42–44
Clueless, 17
cookies for dogs, 18–19
Cooper, Bobb, 13
Crazy, Stupid, Love, 5, 36–37
The Croods, 46

D

Drive, 24

E

Easy A, 33–35

G

Gangster Squad, 46
Ghosts of Girlfriends Past, 29

H

Harrelson, Woody, 30
The Help, 6, 37–42
Heroes, 23
The House Bunny, 29

J

Jones, Allison, 24

M

Marmaduke, 32
MTV Movie Awards, 5, 35
MTV Trailblazer Award, 5–8
Murray, Bill, 30

N

The New Partridge Family, 20–21

P

Panettiere, Hayden, 23
paparazzi, 32
Paper Man, 30–31
The Partridge Family, 19–20
Planes, Trains and Automobiles, 9–10

Project Hollywood 2004, 14–15

R

Radner, Gilda, 10, 43
The Rocker, 27–29

S

Saturday Night Live, 10, 29, 30, 35–36, 41
Savage Agency, 18
Screen Actors Guild (SAG), 22–23
Stockett, Kathryn, 37–39
Stone, Emma
anxiety, 10–11, 36
childhood, family life, 9–17
education, 11–15
fame, 31–32
social life, 44, 45
work ethic, 13–15, 19
Superbad, 24–26, 45

T

Taylor, Tate, 39

W

Wald, Doug, 21
William Morris Agency, 17
The Wind in the Willows, 12–13

Z

Zombieland, 29–31